DISCOVERING AMERICA
★ An Exceptional Nation ★

The United States' Role in the World

Derek Miller

Cavendish
Square

New York

Published in 2019 by Cavendish Square Publishing, LLC
243 5th Avenue, Suite 136, New York, NY 10016

Copyright © 2019 by Cavendish Square Publishing, LLC

First Edition

This publication represents the opinions and views of the author based on
his or her personal experience, knowledge, and research. The information
in this book serves as a general guide only. The author and publisher have
used their best efforts in preparing this book and disclaim liability rising
directly or indirectly from the use and application of this book.

All websites were available and accurate when this book was sent to press.

Library of Congress Cataloging-in-Publication Data

Names: Miller, Derek L., author.
Title: Discovering America : the United States' role in the world / Derek Miller.
Description: New York : Cavendish Square, 2019. | Series: Discovering America:
an exceptional nation | Includes bibliographical references and index.
Identifiers: LCCN 2018027901 (print) | LCCN 2018028045 (ebook) |
ISBN 9781502643599 (ebook) | ISBN 9781502642646 (library bound) |
ISBN 9781502643582 (pbk.)
Subjects: LCSH: United States--Foreign relations--Juvenile literature.
Classification: LCC E183.7 (ebook) | LCC E183.7 .M554 2019 (print) |
DDC 327.73--dc23
LC record available at https://lccn.loc.gov/2018027901

Editorial Director: David McNamara
Editor: Caitlyn Miller
Copy Editor: Rebecca Rohan
Associate Art Director: Alan Sliwinski
Designer: Joe Parenteau
Production Coordinator: Karol Szymczuk
Photo Research: J8 Media

Printed in the United States of America

★ CONTENTS ★

★ ★ ★ ★ ★ ★ ★

★ ★ ★ ★ ★ ★ ★

The Declaration of Independence, signed in 1776, was the first step toward the formation of the United States.

Chapter One

The Birth of the Republic: 1491–1800

★ ★ ★ ★ ★ ★ ★

America's role in the world has been in constant flux for its 243-year history. As a newly independent nation in the 1700s, the United States had limited power compared to the great empires of Europe. Less than a century and a half later, America was the largest economy in the world. By 1991, it was the world's sole superpower after the collapse of the Soviet Union. Since then, the American government has conducted itself as a global leader, responsible for upholding international order.

America's Controversial Role

America's foreign policy is marked by a number of contradictions that have existed since its earliest days.

★ ★ ★ ★ ★ ★ ★

On the one hand, there is a strong tendency toward isolationism—the idea that a country should not be too heavily involved in the affairs of foreign nations. Many Founding Fathers argued for this stance, and it was a strong force in American politics for most of history. The late entry of the country into both World Wars was due to the strong isolationist leanings of the population and politicians at the time.

On the other hand, much of American history is marked by interventionism abroad. Today, the United States has military troops stationed in more than 150 countries around the globe! Earlier in history, the United States directly controlled several foreign countries, such as the Philippines and Cuba. The question of how entangled the United States should be in world affairs has been debated a great deal.

The tension between isolationism and internationalism is not the only controversy in American foreign policy. A second controversy is related to the way that the United States sees itself. Many people have seen the United States as—in the words of Thomas Jefferson—an "Empire of Liberty": an empire that ought to expand and spread freedom and democracy to people around the globe. This idea was behind the rapid expansion of the United States across North America, and it was also one of the guiding principles behind the wars in Iraq and Afghanistan in the twenty-first century under President George W. Bush.

The notion of the United States as a shining example of freedom and peace to the rest of the world is inspiring. But the American government has always been pragmatic. The values of freedom and peace must be balanced with acting in the nation's best interest. Sometimes, the interests of the American government run counter to supporting democracy. These times have resulted in intense political debates over how to act, and national interests have outweighed American values on many occasions.

As we trace America's ever-evolving role in the world, we will look at these tensions and controversies. Isolationism and internationalism have ebbed and flowed depending on both the will of the people and their elected representatives. Meanwhile, the balancing of high ideals and American values with American interests has not always been easy. Often, political parties have not been able to come to agreement on how to proceed. Sometimes, the American people have also been bitterly opposed to American involvement in questionable wars and conflicts.

European Settlers Arrive

The exploration and colonization of the Americas began in 1492. Christopher Columbus, funded by the Spanish crown, reached the islands of the Caribbean. Spain began claiming land and establishing settlements in the New

Christopher Columbus first made landfall in the present-day Bahamas before exploring more of the Caribbean.

World. Other European powers soon laid claim to their own colonies in the Americas. Spain ended up with the lion's share, including most of Central and South America, though France and Great Britain carved out large territories from the expanse of North America. Portugal settled the large territory of Brazil. European countries like the Netherlands, Sweden, and Denmark also colonized parts of the New World. However, those countries never secured the vast swaths of land that Spain, Great Britain, and France did in North America.

The race to claim and colonize the New World was driven by a few factors. The Christian countries of Europe wanted to convert the indigenous people of the Americas to Christianity. They often forced these conversions at gunpoint. European nations also wanted to claim the natural resources of the "new" land they had only just discovered. Huge quantities of gold and silver were extracted and sent across the Atlantic to Europe. Expensive crops like cotton, tobacco, and sugar also grew well in the New World. The production of these crops helped the monarchs of Europe grow rich.

The European powers colonized their territories in different ways. Spain conquered large stretches of territory, some of it rich in gold and silver. This led the Spanish to try to subjugate the indigenous people in order to use their labor. Spanish conquistadors forced the people to convert to Christianity and abide by Spanish laws. Indigenous peoples and slaves worked in mines and fields to produce wealth for Spain. There was a strict caste system, based on one's background and race. Those of Spanish ancestry were at the top. They administered the colonial system for the Spanish monarchy. Slaves and indigenous people were at the bottom, with few rights. The middle was occupied by those of mixed ancestry.

France and the Netherlands took a very different approach. With limited land that lacked gold and silver, they ran their colonies with a light touch. A small number of European colonists and merchants set up trading posts. They grew rich off trading with the Native Americans for goods like furs. These goods were then shipped to Europe.

British colonies took a much more hands-on approach than France and the Netherlands. British colonies were populated by large numbers of people from Great Britain and other European countries. These colonists spread out and settled the land. Rather than incorporating Native

Americans into their society or leaving them alone, they pushed the Native peoples away from British settlements. The indigenous people who had lived on the east coast of North America were forced farther and farther inland.

The Columbian Exchange

Throughout the New World, the arrival of the European settlers was a disaster for the indigenous people. Diseases from Europe spread across the continents. Often, Native Americans would experience a wave of new diseases from Europe before ever meeting a European, as the diseases spread from one indigenous community to the next. Diseases like smallpox, measles, and the flu had never been seen in the New World. This meant that the indigenous population was much more vulnerable than Europeans. Millions of Native Americans died in the waves of epidemics that lasted for centuries.

Disease was only one part of the Columbian Exchange. Columbus's voyage to the New World also sparked a massive transfer of plants, animals, people, and ideas between the Americas and Europe. The exchange took place in both directions: from Europe to the Americas and from the Americas to Europe. European animals like horses, sheep, cattle, and pigs were brought to the Americas for the first time. This radically altered the culture of some Native American tribes. Tribes that had farmed in the same place for generations became nomads on horseback. Roaming across the Great Plains, Native Americans used their new horses to hunt buffalo much more effectively than before.

The Europeans gained access to a cornucopia of new crops. For the first time, potatoes, corn, squash, pumpkins, peppers, and peanuts arrived in Europe. Many soon became staples of the European diet. Tobacco and cocoa beans (used to make chocolate) also came to Europe for the first time. These luxury goods quickly became popular. The exchange of these plants helped spur economic growth around the world. Eventually, the plants from the New World spread from Europe to Asia.

A New Economy

The colonization of the Americas and the Columbian Exchange spurred a series of economic revolutions. These changes went on to shape world history to the present day. They also set the stage for the American Revolution and an independent United States.

The colonization of the Americas resulted in a new system of global trade. Commodities—raw materials like tobacco, cotton, and sugar—were produced in the New World. These commodities were exported to Europe to fuel the appetite for luxury goods (in the case of sugar and tobacco), and the textile industry (in the case of cotton). Meanwhile, European merchants traded various goods like guns, alcohol, and fabric in Africa in return for slaves. The slaves were then transported across the Atlantic and sold in the New World to produce more commodities to be exported to Europe.

This trade circuit is often called the Triangular Trade since the three points of the Americas, Europe, and West Africa form a triangle around which goods flowed. The end result was a vast increase in wealth in Europe and the New World. African leaders, however, were forced into an arms race. They had to sell slaves in order to buy guns from the European merchants to compete with their neighbors doing the same.

Mercantilism and Capitalism

During the Triangular Trade, finished goods from Europe, such as cotton cloth, were exported to British colonies in the Americas. This trade of raw materials from British colonies to Great Britain, where they were used to manufacture finished goods that were sent back to the colonies, underpinned mercantilism. Mercantilism is an economic policy that favors a positive balance of trade. A country's balance of trade is calculated by comparing its imports—the goods that are brought into a country—to its exports—goods sent out of a country to be sold in foreign markets. A positive balance of trade means that the value of a country's exports exceeds the value of its

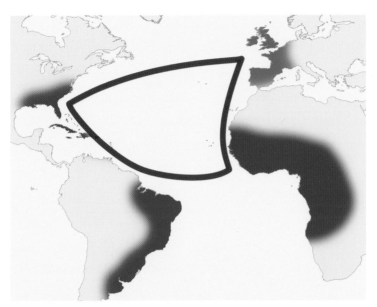

The Triangular Trade had three main routes: from Europe to Africa, from Africa to the Americas, and from the Americas to Europe.

imports. The result of this is an inflow of money, often in the form of gold and silver.

European countries like Great Britain were able to sustain a positive balance of trade through their colonies. They curtailed their colonies' ability to trade with other countries through restrictive laws and tariffs, taxes on the trading of certain goods. One important example of such a law is the Navigation Acts of the middle of the seventeenth century. These British laws forbade British colonies from exporting sugar, tobacco, and indigo to any area outside the control of the British. Trading certain commodities to Dutch, French, or Spanish merchants was illegal. The people of the thirteen colonies chafed under the restrictive laws that were part of mercantilism. In fact, colonists often resorted to smuggling goods to merchants of other countries in order to maximize profits.

The new economic system of mercantilism that dominated Europe between the sixteenth and eighteenth centuries had another effect. It concentrated huge amounts of wealth in the form of goods, silver, and gold in the hands of a new social class of merchants. These merchants invested their wealth in new business ventures and trade. The result was a new economic system, one that dominates the global economy to this day: capitalism. Capitalism is based on private ownership of the means of production, meaning resources like factories and farmland. Capitalism contrasts with economic systems like feudalism and communism where the means of production are owned by the nobility or the government.

The vast wealth that the Triangular Trade created was put in the hands of private merchants rather than just the government. For the first time in history, capitalism spread across Europe and North America as merchants reinvested their wealth.

The French and Indian War

The wealth of the American colonies eventually led to conflict in Europe. The historic rivalry between France and Great Britain was reignited on the shores of America, as both countries expanded across what is now the eastern half of the United States. By 1750, the thirteen colonies of Great Britain spread along the Atlantic Coast. Meanwhile, the colony of New France spread up from New Orleans on the Gulf of Mexico through the center of North America into present-day Canada. The border between these two large colonies was unclear. Both France and Great Britain claimed a large strip of territory along their borders.

The confluence of the Allegheny and Monongahela Rivers was part of the disputed territory. It was a strategic area that each European power wanted for themselves. The French built a fort at the fork of the two rivers: Fort Duquesne. However, a young British military officer, George Washington, was sent to secure the area for Great Britain. He ambushed a small group of French-Canadian soldiers, killing their leader, Joseph Coulon de Villiers de Jumonville, among others.

A larger French force quickly captured Washington and his men. The event was a major incident. It is considered the first battle of the French and Indian War. The French and Indian War is the name for the American theater of the larger Seven Years' War. The Seven Years' War is often called the first true world war. It involved nearly every major European power, and by extension, their colonies across the globe. In the American theater, it pitted the

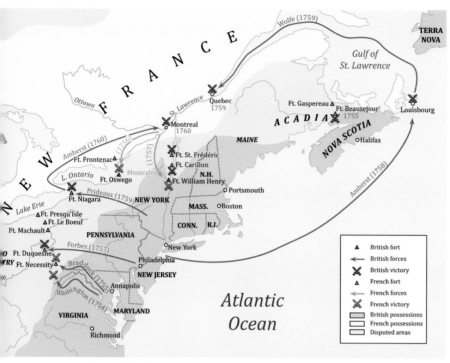

Some of the fighting during the French and Indian War took place in modern-day Canada. This land was ceded by the French to the British after the war.

French against the British. Both sides were also aided by various Native American tribes. The thirteen colonies and New France fought for their respective parent countries.

The French and Indian War lasted eight years. It was a costly war that greatly strained both Great Britain and France. The debts incurred by both countries would have lasting consequences. In the end, Great Britain was victorious. France agreed to cede all territory east of the Mississippi River to the British. This greatly increased the size of the British colonies in North America.

The American Revolutionary War

The British victory in the French and Indian War soon soured relations between Great Britain and the thirteen colonies. After the war ended, King George III issued the Proclamation of 1763. It decreed that all lands west of the Appalachian Mountains were off limits to colonial settlement. The spoils of war were taken away from the colonists who had fought for Great Britain in the Americas. The reason for the proclamation was to improve relations with Native Americans, who were tired of being pushed farther and farther west. But the creation of a vast reserve for Native Americans enraged many colonists who felt entitled to the land.

King George III also wanted the thirteen colonies to help pay for the French and Indian War. Great Britain had undertaken the costly venture of defending the colonies from the French and Indian forces in North America. From Britain's point of view, it was only fair that they help shoulder some of the enormous financial burden this had put on the country. The colonists disagreed. Banned from moving west, they did not want to pay increased taxes for a war they had already fought on behalf of Great Britain.

In 1765, Great Britain passed the Stamp Act. It was the first direct tax on American colonists. Earlier taxes had only been placed on goods, like sugar, that were being brought into the colonies. Paid at ports on goods from outside the colonies, these taxes were less controversial. The Stamp Act required that printed materials, such as pamphlets, wills, and contracts, bear a stamp that was given in exchange for money. The tax was roundly condemned by the colonists. Resistance efforts were organized, and many people refused to pay the tax. They argued there could be no taxation without representation, and the thirteen colonies had no representatives in Parliament in London.

Tensions eventually boiled over. On April 19, 1775, British soldiers tried to confiscate an arms cache. A battle broke out between the soldiers and the local colonial militia. In the end, the British withdrew after suffering several hundred casualties. The Battles of Lexington and Concord were the first clashes of the American Revolution. Many colonists still hoped for a peaceful resolution to the conflict, one that would allow them to remain part of Great Britain. However, this grew less likely as the war intensified. On July 4, 1776, representatives of the thirteen colonies approved the Declaration of Independence. Even though some colonists wished to remain British citizens, most representatives agreed that was no longer possible.

George Washington led the Continental Army against British troops in the colonies. The inexperienced Continental Army seemed no match for the highly experienced British Army, but Continental soldiers were able to avoid defeat. France supported the Continental

American colonists forced British troops to withdraw in the Battles of Lexington and Concord at the beginning of the Revolutionary War.

Army with guns and money informally at first, eager to avenge their defeat in the Seven Years' War and harm their rival Great Britain. In 1778, France officially joined the war and fought the British with their navy and army. Their help was invaluable.

In 1783, the war ended in an American and French victory. Great Britain agreed to recognize the independence of the thirteen colonies. It was a favorable peace deal for the Americans. Great Britain wanted to ensure that there was no deep resentment that might push the colonists to favor France over Great Britain in the future.

A New Republic

The colonists had to organize a new government after declaring their independence. Initially, they drafted the

Articles of Confederation. This document outlined a very loose confederation of states with a weak central government. For the most part, the individual states were expected to govern themselves. The shortcomings of such a weak central government soon became apparent, as it struggled to govern the country.

In 1787, representatives of the states gathered at the Constitutional Convention. They drafted the United States Constitution to replace the Articles of Confederation. The Constitution created a stronger federal government that had supremacy over state governments in some affairs. The new federal government could levy taxes, make treaties with foreign countries, and maintain an army and navy.

The Constitution balanced the interests of small states and large states by creating a bicameral (two-chamber) legislature, composed of the Senate and the House of Representatives. Each state is represented by the same number of senators, while the number of representatives in the House is determined by a state's population. The Constitution also divided the government into three branches: the legislative, executive, and judicial. The legislative branch is responsible for writing laws, the executive for enforcing them, and the judicial for interpreting them in court. Congress, composed of the Senate and the House, makes up the legislative branch. The executive branch is headed by the president, who also leads the armed forces, and contains the departments and agencies of the federal government. The judicial branch is made up of the judges and courts.

The new government was based on the ideals of the Enlightenment. The most famous expression of these ideals is found in the Declaration of Independence: "We hold these truths to be self-evident, that all men are created equal, that they are endowed by their Creator with certain unalienable Rights, that among these are Life, Liberty and the pursuit of Happiness." The idea that all men are equal was not universally accepted at the time. Aristocrats and commoners were often governed by different laws in Europe. The Constitution also drew a strict separation between church and state. This, too, was alien to many European countries.

One of the most important aspects of the Constitution was its commitment to a republican system of government. In a republic, the power is held by the people. The opening words of the Constitution, "We the people," highlight this fact. It was a bold statement of the importance of individual citizens in a world where monarchs and the aristocrats who supported them controlled most governments.

A Model of Government

From its founding, the United States had a unique role in the world as a representative of personal freedom and democratic government. In his inaugural address,

The Constitution of the United States is a broad outline of a system of government. Many intricacies of how the government should function were left vague, including foreign policy. It is clear that both the Senate and

George Washington was president from 1789 to 1797.

the president have significant powers when it comes to dealing with foreign countries. The Constitution states that the Senate must ratify any treaty. But the powers of the president are less clear.

George Washington was responsible for shaping many aspects of the presidency through his example—or precedent. He was very aware of this responsibility. Before taking the oath of office, he frequently commented, "I walk on untrodden ground." Washington's first major foreign-policy challenge was creating an agreement with the Creek Nation in present-day Florida. Washington went to consult the Senate before sending negotiators, but they proved difficult to work with. Washington stormed out. He decided that treaty negotiations would take place without advice from the Senate. After Washington's negotiators had penned a treaty with the Creek Nation, it was sent to the Senate for ratification.

This set an important precedent for foreign policy. The Senate plays some role, but the president has sweeping powers to act independently. The Senate must consent to major decisions like treaties and formal declarations of war, but its advisory role is quite limited.

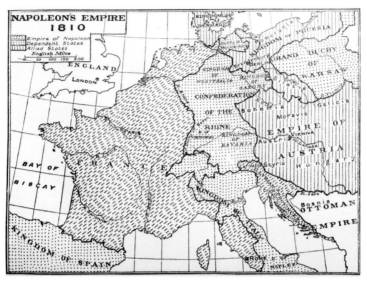

At the height of its power, the influence of Napoleon's First French Empire spread across the modern-day Netherlands, Belgium, Switzerland, Spain, Germany, and Italy.

George Washington said, "the preservation of the sacred fire of liberty, and the destiny of the Republican model of Government, are justly considered as deeply, perhaps as finally staked, on the experiment entrusted to the hands of the American people." Through its example, the United States has spread liberty and the republican model of government across the globe.

This was true in the new republic's earliest days. In 1789, France was gripped by the French Revolution. The country was deep in debt due to the loss of the Seven Years' War and the expense it incurred supporting the thirteen colonies during the American Revolutionary War. People looking to the example of the United States tried to overthrow the monarchy and create a new republic. The French king lost power and was executed. After years of turmoil, Napoleon seized control of the country. His rise marked the end of the republican government, as he gradually took total control of the country. He waged a series of wars and briefly conquered nearly all of Europe, except Great Britain. In doing so, he spread the Enlightenment ideals of liberty and equality across Europe.

The small Caribbean island nation of Haiti also looked to the United States for inspiration. In 1791, the slaves of the French colony rebelled. A bloody twelve-year revolution followed. Haiti succeeded in ending French control of the island but failed to set up a stable republic. The example of the United States was a powerful motivator for people seeking freedom in both the Americas and in Europe.

Preventing War with Britain

During the terms of the first two presidents, George Washington and John Adams, the focus of American foreign policy was on peaceful free trade. When the French Revolutionary War broke out, Washington issued the Proclamation of Neutrality. In it, he stated that the United States would "adopt and pursue a conduct friendly and impartial toward the belligerent powers." In other words, the United States would not take sides in the conflict. It was a move toward isolationism. The United States chose not to intervene in the foreign war. However, Washington's decision was also driven by the desire to trade with all belligerents. By not taking sides, the United States hoped to stay close to both France and Great Britain and its allies.

Despite American neutrality, British ships soon seized American merchant vessels trying to trade with France. Britain was embargoing the continent, cutting it off from overseas trade. Great Britain even forcibly recruited some American sailors from ships it seized, a practice known as impressment.

These British actions created a crisis. It seemed that war with Britain was possible. George Washington sent statesman John Jay to negotiate an end to the practice. The resulting treaty was deeply unpopular with the American people. Great Britain agreed to evacuate a number of forts it still manned in American territory. However, American trading rights were limited in the British West Indies. Great Britain was even allowed to seize American merchant vessels bound for France, so long as it paid for their cargo.

The Democratic-Republican Party, including Thomas Jefferson, bitterly opposed the treaty. They argued that it weakened American sovereignty—the power of a country to rule itself. The Federalist Party argued that it was necessary to prevent a war with Great Britain. In the end, the treaty was narrowly approved the Senate and signed by Washington. War with Great Britain was avoided.

The United States' Role in the World

George Washington's Advice

On September 19, 1796, George Washington had his farewell address published in a Philadelphia newspaper. He informed the public of his decision not to seek a third term as president of the United States. By doing so, he set a precedent that every American president except for Franklin D. Roosevelt would follow. (The Twenty-Second Amendment, which established a two-term limit for presidents, was ratified in 1951.)

Washington's farewell address also included a great deal of advice for the new country and its citizens. Washington urged caution in binding the fate of the United States with foreign powers in Europe: "The great rule of conduct for us in regard to foreign nations is in extending our commercial relations, to have with them as little political connection as possible." This isolationism was possible because of the vast geographic distance between the United States and Europe. He wrote, "Our detached and distant situation invites and enables us to pursue a different course"—outside of European alliances and wars.

The address was a strong defense of an isolationist foreign policy apart from trade. It is cited to this day by those who think the United States is too involved with the rest of the world.

The Battle of the Little Bighorn, sometimes known as Custer's Last Stand, was just one of many battles fought against Native Americans during the 1800s.

Chapter Two

America Looks West: 1800–1877

★ ★ ★ ★ ★ ★ ★

Between 1800 and 1877, the United States spread across North America at an extraordinary pace. Starting from the land east of the Mississippi River, it had reached its current borders in the continental United States by 1853. Renewed conflict with Great Britain and the devastating Civil War also defined this period. The ability of the United States to navigate these challenges and expand across the continent positioned it to be a world power in the coming years.

The Louisiana Purchase

The first major territorial expansion of the United States was the Louisiana Purchase. After the French and Indian

★ ★ ★ ★ ★ ★ ★

The Louisiana Purchase doubled the size of the United States and made further westward expansion possible.

War concluded, France had ceded its vast territory west of the Mississippi River to Spain. In 1800, Napoleon forced Spain to give this land back to France.

This placed the United States in a difficult position. A great deal of American trade flowed down the Mississippi River through New Orleans. Previously, an agreement had been signed with Spain giving American merchants access to the important port of New Orleans. France was not bound by this agreement.

President Thomas Jefferson sent his close political ally James Monroe to negotiate with France. He was instructed to open the route to trade. Ideally, Monroe would buy both New Orleans and the territory of Florida in the east. This

The United States' Role in the World

would make conflict with France less likely in the future. When Monroe arrived in France, he was informed that Napoleon wished to sell the entire territory of Louisiana to the United States. Napoleon needed money to pursue his war in Europe, and his dream of an American empire seemed out of reach. The sale of the territory would double the size of the United States.

After negotiations, Monroe agreed to pay $15 million for the land. Unfortunately, there was no provision in the Constitution about buying foreign territory. Jefferson had always argued for a strict view of constitutionality and for a presidency with limited power. Nevertheless, he agreed to the Louisiana Purchase rather than pass up the opportunity. The deal went through, and five months after it had taken place, it was ratified by the Senate. The United States had doubled in size and was positioned to expand still farther west.

The War of 1812

Early American foreign policy was aimed at promoting free trade and avoiding involvement in European wars. These two issues became impossible to reconcile in 1812. The war between Great Britain and Napoleonic France still dragged on. Napoleon controlled nearly all mainland Europe. Britain was embargoing Europe to strike at France's economy. The United States was caught in the

Thomas Jefferson's tenure as the third president was dominated by foreign affairs. His political career was marked by a deep skepticism toward foreign wars, the executive power of the president, and the federal government in general. He firmly believed that the states ought to be left to govern themselves. However, circumstances forced him to lead the country through a series of foreign crises.

In 1801, Tripolitania, one of the Barbary States in North Africa, declared war on the United States. Previously, the United States had paid tribute, a sort of bribe, to the Barbary States so that their pirates would avoid attacking American ships. However, the deal broke down, and Jefferson dispatched the American navy to protect American ships near Europe. The war was a mixed success. In the end, the United States paid a ransom for hostages held in Africa and resumed paying tribute. However, it demonstrated that the United States would fight back if its commercial interests were threatened.

Jefferson also oversaw the passage of the Embargo Act by Congress in 1807. The law embargoed, or forbade trade, with both Great Britain and France due to the impressment of American sailors. It was intended to force Great Britain and France to recognize the United States' right to trade freely, but it failed. Neither European power was willing to budge, as they waged a war against one another in Europe. Jefferson was left to police the restrictive embargo and try to stop American smugglers. The American economy suffered terribly. It is remembered as a massive exercise of federal power by a president who spent his career fighting for a smaller federal government.

Thomas Jefferson was president from 1801 to 1809.

middle. American vessels that visited Britain were labeled enemies by France and vice versa. Britain's practice of impressment against American sailors continued. Jay's Treaty and Jefferson's Embargo Act proved unable to prevent the coming conflict.

On June 18, 1812, with the support of Congress, President James Madison signed a declaration of war against Great Britain. It was justified under the slogan "Free trade and sailor's rights." American forces invaded Canada, which was still a British colony and the only military objective that the United States could easily reach. At first, the British were too distracted by Napoleon to respond with much force. However, the British did form an alliance with Native American tribes in Canada to raid the United States, and Canadian militias resisted the invasion.

In 1814, Napoleon was finally defeated and sent into exile. Great Britain was free to turn its full attention to the United States. The British raided the coast of Maryland. Washington, DC, fell to British forces. The United States Capitol, where Congress meets, and the White House were burned to the ground. Nevertheless, the British failed to take Baltimore, the third-largest city in the United States and an important port in Maryland. Francis Scott Key wrote "The Star-Spangled Banner" as he watched the battle for the city.

Another important battle of the War of 1812 was the Battle of New Orleans. It was fought after the war ended but before news had reached soldiers on either side. The Battle of New Orleans was a surprising American victory. General Andrew Jackson managed to hold the city against a much larger British force. While it had little military significance, since the war was over, the battle made Jackson a national hero and paved his way to the presidency.

The Americans and British ultimately signed a peace treaty in 1814. Neither side gained anything from the treaty, and the Americans could not secure a promise to end the practice of impressment. The war was momentous in some ways, though. It was the last time Native Americans would be used by European powers to wage war on their behalf. It was also the last war the United States would wage against Great Britain, and the last time the fledgling nation was clearly less powerful than its adversary during a war.

The Monroe Doctrine

In the 1800s, the United States looked to broaden its territory across North America and its influence across the entire Western Hemisphere, including Central and South America. The period of European domination of the Americas was ending. Between 1808 and 1823, nearly every Spanish and Portuguese colony in the New World declared its independence. The Americas was now made up of mostly independent states, with the notable exceptions of British Canada and Spanish Cuba and Puerto Rico.

As European power in the Western Hemisphere waned and American confidence grew, President James Monroe gave his 1823 State of the Union address to Congress. In the speech, he outlined a bold new vision of American foreign policy. It later came to be known as the Monroe Doctrine, and it has been one of the most influential ideas in American foreign policy throughout history. Monroe said in his speech:

> *With the existing colonies or dependencies of any European power we have not interfered and shall not interfere. But with the Governments who have declared their independence and maintain it, and whose independence we have, on great consideration and on just principles, acknowledged, we could not view any interposition for the purpose of oppressing them, or controlling in any other manner their destiny, by any European power in any other light than as the manifestation of an unfriendly disposition toward the United States.*

In other words, the United States would leave the remaining European colonies in peace. However, the Western Hemisphere was off limits to further European colonization or influence. Any attempt to interfere in the Americas would be viewed as an "unfriendly" act toward the United States.

The Monroe Doctrine had little practical effect at the time, but future presidents expanded its meaning and continued to follow it. In the 1860s, the United States opposed a French intervention in Mexico. In the first half of the twentieth century, the doctrine was expanded to mean that Latin America was in the sphere of influence of the United States. American military forces intervened in the countries of the region repeatedly.

Manifest Destiny

After the Louisiana Purchase, Americans began moving West with growing frequency. By 1840, about 40 percent of Americans lived west of the Appalachian Mountains. The West was associated with the American ideals of freedom and land ownership. People born in states along the East Coast packed up their belongings and moved west, seeking economic opportunities.

This westward expansion came to be seen as a moral imperative, or duty. Many people felt the United States was meant to spread freedom and their style of representative government west across the continent. This idea had inspired Jefferson's Louisiana Purchase, and it would continue to inspire American politicians and citizens.

In 1845, journalist John O'Sullivan coined the term "Manifest Destiny" to describe this national drive west. The word "manifest" means clear or obvious. Manifest Destiny meant that the march of the United States westward was

This famous 1872 painting, *The Spirit of the Frontier*, depicts the westward migration of Americans.

the country's obvious destiny. O'Sullivan imagined this as the peaceful spread of democracy and freedom, but reality would be quite different.

The nation's expansion westward was bloody, contentious, and ultimately led to the Civil War that ripped the country apart. Force was used to seize territory from Mexico, dividing the American public. Native Americans were driven from their lands. But the most divisive issue in the United States was the spread of slavery.

Slavery had existed in the United States since its colonial days. Agriculture, especially in the South, relied on the labor of enslaved Africans and later their descendants. While slavery was practiced in the North in early American history, it gradually decreased in popularity. A division between "free states" (states without slaves) in the North and "slave states" in the South began to dominate American politics. The South grew convinced that the North would eventually try to end the institution of slavery. Meanwhile, abolitionists, people who opposed the institution, grew increasingly frustrated as slavery spread across parts of the West.

As the country expanded west, the addition of new states to the country threatened the delicate balance between free and slave states. Both sides, those for and against slavery, were bitterly opposed to the other gaining a large majority in Congress. Resolving which new states should be free states and which should be slave states increased tensions on both sides. The matter of slavery was finally decided by the American Civil War, which devastated the country and ended the institution once and for all.

The Mexican-American War

President James K. Polk was elected to office in 1844. During his campaign, he promised to expand the United States westward. Part of his plan was the acquisition of

The green area on this map was given by Mexico to the United States in the aftermath of the Mexican-American War.

California—then a part of Mexico. He made an offer to the Mexican government to buy the land, but they refused. As a result, he sent General Zachary Taylor and an American army to the disputed border between the two countries in attempt to spark a war. His efforts paid off. A skirmish broke out between Mexican and American troops, and Polk demanded a declaration of war from Congress.

On May 13, 1846, Congress declared war on Mexico. Taylor invaded Mexico while other American armies swept through what is today the American Southwest. Back then, it was the territory that Polk hoped to gain from the war. The Mexican Army was outmatched by the American military, but the war was still costly and bloody. By its end,

The United States' Role in the World

more than 13,200 American soldiers and 25,000 Mexicans, including many civilians, had died in the struggle.

The war was controversial in the United States. In the Senate, Henry Clay roundly condemned the war, "This is no war of defense, but one unnecessary and of offensive aggression." Likewise, the Massachusetts Legislature passed a resolution calling for its citizens to obstruct the war effort:

> *A war of conquest, so hateful in its objects, so wanton, unjust, and unconstitutional in its origin and character, must be regarded as a war against freedom, against humanity, against justice, against the Union, against the Constitution, and against the Free States; and that a regard for the true interests and the highest honor of the country, not less than the impulses of Christian duty, should arouse all good citizens to join in efforts to arrest this gigantic crime, by withholding supplies, or other voluntary contributions, for its further prosecution; by calling for the withdrawal of our army within the established limits of the United States; and in every just way aiding the country to retreat from the disgraceful position of aggression which it now occupies towards a weak, distracted neighbor and sister republic.*

But opponents of the war could not stop the bloodshed. Mexico's capital was occupied by American soldiers, and it was forced to the negotiating table. The United States was able to dictate the terms of the Treaty of Guadalupe Hidalgo. For just $15 million, Mexico was forced to give the United States a third of its territory. This included the present-day states of California, Nevada, Arizona, Utah, New Mexico, and parts of Colorado and Texas.

Many Americans had tried to stop the unjust war. Abraham Lincoln, then a young congressman, spoke out against the war and was not reelected as a result. But in the end, American interests won out over its values. The fact that Mexico was a neighboring republic that shared the same values did not save it from being the target of an aggressive, expansionist war.

Conflict with Native Americans

As European colonists settled the New World, they came into conflict with Native Americans. While these conflicts occurred throughout American history, there were a number of important events between the years of 1800 and 1877. The spread of the United States across the country brought settlers, and then American soldiers, into many conflicts against Native Americans who wished to keep their lands. Previous wars had often seen the Native Americans retreat west out of the United States. However, during this period, the United States expanded all the way to the Pacific Ocean, making escape impossible.

The United States' Role in the World

Many different wars were fought by the United States against Native American tribes in the West. Collectively, these are known as the Indian Wars. They were often brutal and merciless. Prisoners were rarely taken. A number of times American soldiers massacred not only Native American men who were unarmed but also women and children. Settlers encroaching on Native American lands were also killed.

One Indian War was the Colorado War, which was fought between 1863 and 1865. It pitted the Cheyenne and Arapaho tribes against white settlers. Local militias did much of the fighting rather than the American army. The war began with the Sand Creek Massacre. A peaceful village of Native Americans was relocated to an area designated by the US Army. The Native Americans were supposed to be under American protection after having agreed to move to a smaller reservation. Instead, they were massacred by American cavalry. At least 150 were killed, most of them women and children. Their corpses were mutilated, and the militia kept pieces of their bodies as trophies. Native American warriors retaliated in what became known as the Colorado War. It was one of many wars that marked American expansion into the West.

In addition to the Indian Wars in the West, the 1800s were also the period of forced relocation. Between 1830 and 1850, tribes that had called the East Coast their home for generations were forced to walk west to reservations. White Americans wanted the land that they lived on in the Southeast. The Cherokee, Choctaw, Chickasaw, Seminole, and Creek people all met this fate on a forced march known today as the Trail of Tears. Tens of thousands were forced to move west. They were exposed to the elements and disease on their long march. Thousands perished.

The United States' treatment of Native Americans in this period was a time when selfish national interests won out over American values. By the end, Native Americans were forced onto reservations where they could no longer practice

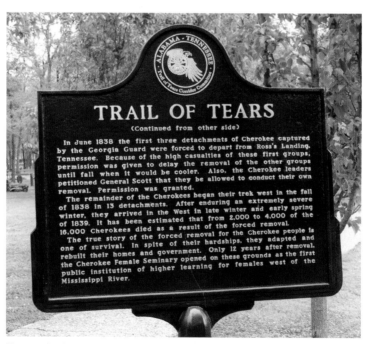

Thousands of Native Americans died when they were forced by the government to march across the United States.

their traditional ways of life. The desire to appropriate Native American lands outweighed the principled arguments of some Americans at the time: that all people are equal, and the rights of Native Americans must be respected.

Interventions in Asia

After reaching the shores of the Pacific Ocean, the United States looked to distant Asia in the East. The spread of American trade and influence into Asia was seen as a part of Manifest Destiny. American merchant ships needed open ports in the region to facilitate trade. The steam-powered vessels of the time were powered by burning coal. As a result, they had to stop regularly at coaling stations to resupply.

Japan, at the eastern edge of Asia, was a natural location to build coaling stations. However, the country had been closed to Western merchants since 1693. Attempts to spread Christianity to the islands by missionaries had led to the expulsion of all Europeans. In 1852, President Millard Fillmore commissioned Commodore Matthew Perry to lead an expedition to open the nation to trade.

Through a combination of gifts and shows of naval force, Perry succeeded. Japan agreed to open two ports to American ships so that they could resupply there. The Japanese also agreed to shelter and return shipwrecked

American sailors who landed on their shores. It was a momentous occasion that shaped world history. After gradually opening up to the West, Japan industrialized and became a world power over the coming century.

Other American expeditions to Asia at the time were less successful. An expedition sent to Korea to begin trade and relations between the two countries was met with gunfire from shore. American troops then landed and engaged Korean forces in battle when no apology for the gunfire was forthcoming. In the end, three Americans and more than two hundred Koreans died. The Korean government refused to negotiate with the Americans after the bloody encounter.

The Civil War

The deepening rift between North and South that sparked the Civil War had many causes. The debate over states' rights, nationalism (a fierce pride among a people) among Southerners and Northerners, and economic differences between the agrarian South and the industrialized North all contributed to the conflict. Nonetheless, the primary cause was the debate over slavery.

From the earliest days of the United States, slavery had been a dividing issue. When the Constitution was written, some states hoped the institution would be banned, but

The Battle of Bull Run, the first of the Civil War, was a bloody Confederate victory. The outcome made it clear that the war would not be over quickly.

Southern states refused to entertain this idea. Instead, the Constitution contained the three-fifths compromise. Slaves would count as three-fifths of a person when determining how many representatives each state had in the House.

As the United States spread west, slavery continued to divide the nation. Political crisis after political crisis ensued, as Southerners pushed for slavery in all new territories while Northerners argued it should be banned in them. A series of compromises divided the West, with slavery allowed in the southern states and territories while it was banned in the northern ones.

War and the Constitution

The Constitution divides the power to wage war between the legislative and executive branches of government. This is in line with the Constitution's checks and balances on the powers of the three branches of government. The division of war powers limits the ability of either the legislative or executive branch of government to independently pursue a war. Congress is responsible for both declaring war and funding the war. The president, the head of the executive branch, is responsible for directing the military as commander in chief.

Congress has only officially declared war eleven times in American history, even though the military has engaged in many more conflicts. The first declared war was the War of 1812 and the last was World War II between 1941 and 1945. Thomas Jefferson's Barbary War was not a declared war, nor were the modern-day wars in Afghanistan and Iraq.

Some conflicts that were not formally declared wars had the support of Congress. For instance, Congress passed a law giving Jefferson permission to undertake military actions during the Barbary War. However, sometimes a president has not sought congressional approval to engage in a conflict. For example, Barack Obama ordered the bombing of the African country of Libya in 2011 with no authorization from Congress.

The US Navy fought in Tripoli during the First Barbary War.

Many major wars in American history have been fought with no declaration of war in the twentieth and twenty-first century. These include the Vietnam War, the Iraq War, and the war in Afghanistan. This has led some politicians and citizens to worry that the president has too much power to use the military unilaterally. However, usually the president has the consent of Congress when waging these undeclared wars.

With the election of Abraham Lincoln, the South feared that their cause was lost. Despite the fact that Lincoln said he would not push for the abolition of slavery in the South, eleven states seceded from the country. They established the Confederate States of America. Lincoln refused to acknowledge their independence, and the Civil War began.

The war lasted four years, and it had terrible consequences. The Union blockaded the Confederacy and waged total war, ripping up railroad tracks and burning vast swaths of the South. Battle after battle saw more than six hundred thousand American soldiers die. On January 1, 1863, Lincoln issued the Emancipation Proclamation and made it clear that if the Union won, slavery would end. One important reason he did this was to discourage intervention by France or Great Britain on the side of the Confederacy. Fighting a war to save slavery was not a popular idea in Europe. France and Great Britain had outlawed the institution decades before.

In the end, the Union's superior economy and greater population led to military victory. The Confederacy surrendered, and the Thirteenth Amendment was ratified, banning slavery. The United States had turned a corner in its struggle to fulfill the Declaration of Independence's claim that "All men are created equal."

The Civil War was a momentous occasion not only in North America, but also across the world. In the

1860s, the United States was the only major power with a representative government. The French Revolution had failed to form a lasting republic. Two groups in France, Bonapartists and monarchists, were still locked in a struggle for absolute power. The Civil War could have spelled the end of the American experiment and its shining example of liberty to the world. At the beginning of the war, monarchists in Europe predicted that they had survived the crisis that began with the American Revolution. A wave of republican revolutions in Europe in 1848 had been put down, and the United States was being torn apart from within. European powers also descended on the Western Hemisphere, as the United States was occupied and unable to defend the Monroe Doctrine. Spain invaded the Dominican Republic, its former colony, and France installed a French ruler as Emperor of Mexico. These efforts failed once European powers realized that the Union would win the war and be able to enforce the Monroe Doctrine. The Union victory meant that the flame of liberty would not be extinguished.

The Ford Model T was the first affordable automobile. Its cost was kept low thanks to new innovations like the assembly line. The innovations of the Second Industrial Revolution made the United States an economic superpower.

Chapter Three

A World Power Rises: 1877–1945

★ ★ ★ ★ ★ ★ ★

By the end of World War II in 1945, the United States was a superpower. It had eclipsed the European powers of France and Great Britain that once dominated North America. Its economy was the largest in the world, and its military was matched only by the Soviet Union. This turn of events was due to the rapid economic growth and industrialization of the republic. The United States also became an international power due to its participation in both world wars. Nonetheless, from 1877 to 1945, the country struggled to find its place in international affairs. It wavered between building a colonial empire abroad, isolationism, and taking a leading role in the world.

★ ★ ★ ★ ★ ★ ★

The Second Industrial Revolution

The United States' power was largely economic at first. By 1890, it had surpassed the old great powers of Europe to become the largest economy in the world. This was largely due to the Second Industrial Revolution, which took place between 1870 and 1914 and was a period of rapid industrialization.

Factories sprang up across the country, particularly in cities in the North, such as Chicago and New York City. Technologies like the telephone and electric lighting made production much more efficient than in the past. These factories also brought jobs with them. Economic opportunity brought people from rural areas into the city. New opportunities even drew immigrants from across the globe, especially from Europe. This rapid urbanization increased America's labor force.

Stronger ties between states from coast to coast also led to growth. The transcontinental railroad was completed in 1869. It linked California and the East Coast. Along its length, new towns and cities sprang up to take advantage of the opportunities it offered. Additionally, the telephone allowed companies to communicate across the country, making them more efficient than ever before.

Innovations in how work was done also helped the United States outstrip other countries. For instance, in

1913, Henry Ford installed the first assembly line in an automobile factory. Workers were responsible for one small part or task of making a car. When all their efforts were combined, they had made a car much more efficiently than Ford's competitors.

The result of all these advances was cheaper goods and more purchasing power for workers. Standards of living increased across the country, although the gap between the rich and the poor did as well. The middle class also grew, as more and more educated managers were needed to help run companies. This new prosperity set the stage for greater involvement in foreign affairs abroad.

American Imperialism

In the late nineteenth century and early twentieth century, the United States went through a brief period of imperialism. Imperialism is the policy of expanding a country's territory and influence through force. It is often a violent proposition and involves occupying the lands of foreign people. Imperialism was justified by the belief that such efforts would "civilize" the indigenous people of the invaded areas. These ideas and the empire-building that they supported were not uniquely American. At the time, European powers were dividing up the continents of Africa and Asia and gathering the spoils. The topic of imperialism was also deeply divisive in American politics. Many politicians did not support it, citing the idea that America ought to be an example of liberty and democracy, not expansionism.

The Annexation of Hawaii

For most of the 1800s, Hawaii was ruled by a monarch of the indigenous people. It was a system popular with Hawaiians and governed by a constitution. Nonetheless, on January 17, 1893, the monarchy was overthrown by a group of businessmen who wished to join the United States. US Marines from a nearby warship lent the necessary military force for the coup with the backing of President Benjamin Harrison. He signed a treaty to annex Hawaii with the new government. However, before the Senate ratified it, Grover Cleveland was sworn in as president.

Cleveland opposed the annexation of the nation. He gave an impassioned speech to Congress before ending the annexation attempt:

> *If national honesty is to be disregarded and a desire for territorial extension or dissatisfaction with a form of government not our own ought to regulate our conduct, I have entirely misapprehended the mission and character of our Government and the behavior which the conscience of our people demands of their public servants.*

It was a stinging rebuke of those who were for annexation. Cleveland argued that it was against the very mission of the United States to annex a country for territorial expansion. He implied his opponents must have misapprehended—or misunderstood—the United States' role in the world to suggest the annexation of Hawaii.

Cleveland's principled stand only delayed the matter. In 1897, William McKinley became president. The same year, he signed a treaty of annexation. It was the first time that the United States annexed a distant land of independent people, but it was not the last.

The Spanish-American War

At the end of the nineteenth century, Cuba was locked in a struggle for independence from Spain. It was one of Spain's last remaining colonies in the New World. The conflict threatened to draw in the United States, which had strong business ties to the island. In 1898, McKinley sent the USS *Maine* to Havana—the capital of Cuba—to protect American citizens and interests. But on February 15, 1898, the warship mysteriously exploded in the harbor.

Some American newspapers blamed Spain for the explosion. The American public supported the Cuban calls for independence and called for war. War broke out when Congress issued an ultimatum demanding a Spanish withdrawal from Cuba. Anti-imperialists in Congress passed the Teller Amendment, which promised the United States would not annex Cuba. The war lasted less than four months. Spain was soundly defeated on the sea and on land.

After the war, the United States annexed Puerto Rico, Guam, and the Philippines—a large nation home to more than seven million people in Asia. Cuba was not annexed, as the Teller Amendment promised. However, the Platt Amendment was passed by Congress to govern American-Cuban affairs. Its purpose was to protect Cuban independence. To do so, it restricted Cuba's ability to make treaties with other countries and issue public debt. In effect, Cuba was restricted from being a sovereign country.

War soon broke out in the Philippines. The country's inhabitants desired independence, not to be a colony of yet another foreign power. Nationalists—people who desire independence for their homeland—took up arms. The United States violently put down the uprising. Four thousand American soldiers and sixteen thousand Filipino soldiers died. More than 250,000 Filipino civilians perished in the chaos. It was a reminder of the cost of empire. (The Philippines became fully independent from the United States in 1946.)

Theodore Roosevelt

During the Battle of San Juan Hill in Cuba, Theodore Roosevelt became a war hero for leading his men in a charge against a Spanish position. He joined McKinley's presidential ticket in the 1900 race as vice president. Their opponent was William Jennings Bryan, a fierce critic of the imperialist posture that McKinley adopted, which Roosevelt supported. A campaign speech from the time captures Bryan's viewpoint:

> *A republic cannot be an empire, for a republic rests upon the theory that the government derive their powers from the consent of the governed and colonialism violates this theory … Our experiment in colonialism has been unfortunate. Instead of profit, it has brought loss. Instead of strength, it has brought weakness. Instead of glory, it has brought humiliation.*

McKinley won the election, but he was assassinated in 1901. Roosevelt ascended to the presidency. He was a fierce advocate for American imperialism. In 1903, he sent American soldiers to aid a Colombian rebel in founding the country of Panama. The purpose was to secure land for the construction of a canal linking the Atlantic and Pacific Oceans through Central America. With American aid, the revolution succeeded, and Roosevelt achieved his aim. But the move was controversial. It was a clear violation of another country's sovereignty driven by American self-interest.

In 1904, Roosevelt issued the Roosevelt Corollary to the Monroe Doctrine. In part, it read, "in the Western

Theodore Roosevelt greatly expanded America's role in the world, as well as presidential powers at home.

The United States' Role in the World

Hemisphere the adherence of the United States to the Monroe Doctrine may force the United States, however reluctantly, in flagrant cases of such wrongdoing or impotence, to the exercise of an international police power." In other words, the United States reserved the right to intervene in countries throughout the Western Hemisphere if it disapproved of their actions. It was a great expansion of American influence across the globe.

World War I

Despite its frequent interventions in the Western Hemisphere and Asia, the United States still followed a policy of noninvolvement in Europe. This policy was put to the test in 1914. On June 28, Archduke Franz Ferdinand was assassinated by a nationalist who wanted independence for his country. Ferdinand was the heir to the throne of the Austro-Hungarian Empire that ruled over many different European peoples and was a world power at the time.

This one event sparked a worldwide war like the world had never seen before. Austria-Hungary blamed neighboring Serbia for the attack and issued an ultimatum to the country. The ultimatum was impossible for a sovereign country to accept. It called for Austria-Hungary to conduct its own investigation in Serbia. Russia, Serbia's close ally, promised to aid Serbia in the event of war.

Meanwhile, Germany was obligated to come to the aid of Austria-Hungary. France and Great Britain were treaty-bound to defend Russia.

When Serbia rejected the ultimatum, the nations of Europe were led to war. France, Great Britain, and Russia—the Allied Powers—faced off against Germany and Austria-Hungary—the Central Powers. The conflict also involved their colonies, which stretched across nearly all of Africa, much of Asia, and even into North America since Canada was still a part of Great Britain.

Technological innovations made the front lines of the war static. Machine guns, barbed wire, and poison gas led to a system of trenches that resulted in a stalemate. Nonetheless, the war was still incredibly deadly. Millions of men fought and died in trenches over the same small areas of ground between France and Germany. France and Great Britain brought soldiers from their colonies across the world to fight at the front.

President Woodrow Wilson initially followed in the tradition of George Washington and cautioned neutrality. The American people largely supported this view. But public sentiment and Wilson's opinion slowly changed as the war in Europe continued. Germany was blockaded by Great Britain and unable to challenge the British fleet. Germany's only means of striking back was submarines. Therefore, Germany began sinking and capturing merchant

Technological advances made World War I incredibly deadly.

vessels to interfere with British and French commerce. In 1915, Germany sank the ocean liner RMS *Lusitania*, killing more than 1,100 civilians, including 120 Americans. The United States was outraged.

Wilson gradually became convinced that the United States should intervene. He argued that defeating Germany and Austria-Hungary—neither of which had a representative government—would make the world safer for democracy. In 1917, Germany adopted a policy of unrestricted submarine warfare. Any vessel approaching Great Britain or France could be sunk without warning. It broke previous promises to the United States that Germany

The Zimmerman Telegram

In 1917, the German Foreign Secretary Arthur Zimmerman sent a secret, coded telegram to the German Ambassador to Mexico. It read in part:

> We intend to begin unrestricted submarine warfare on the first of February. We shall endeavor in spite of this to keep the United States neutral. In the event of this not succeeding, we make Mexico a proposal of alliance on the following basis: make war together, generous financial support and an understanding on our part that Mexico is to reconquer the lost territory in Texas, New Mexico, and Arizona.

A Mexican invasion of the United States would distract America from the European theater. Germany then thought it could win the war quickly. However, the Mexican government concluded that Mexico could not hope to win a war against the United States, and the territory it might gain was inhabited by large numbers of Americans who would resist their annexation by Mexico.

Despite the Mexican refusal of the offer, the telegram was hugely important. British intelligence services decoded the telegram, and its contents helped convince the American people that they should join World War I.

would give warning before sinking ships so that crews could escape. On April 6, 1917, Congress declared war against Germany.

The United States contributed money, supplies, and soldiers to the war. While the number of American soldiers who fought was modest compared to the other belligerents, it was enough to turn the tide of the war. The doughboys, as American soldiers were called, helped break the stalemate on the front between France and Germany. On November 11, 1918, an armistice—or agreement to end the fighting—was signed.

Woodrow Wilson and The League of Nations

President Wilson was heavily involved in the peace process that followed World War I. At the beginning of 1918, he had delivered a speech outlining his Fourteen Points. They were meant to guarantee world peace going forward and make the World War I "the war to end war." Wilson wanted to guarantee free trade, open seas, liberty for occupied countries, and an association of nations that could resolve disputes between individual countries. It was to be called the League of Nations.

The most ambitious of Wilson's plans was the League of Nations, although he did not invent the idea. The League was meant to secure world peace by overseeing

Woodrow Wilson tried to ensure that World War I would be "the war to end war."

The United States' Role in the World

disarmament and resolving conflicts between nations. It saw some limited success in resolving border disputes, but it was hamstrung by the refusal of the United States to join. Despite Wilson's support, Congress refused to ratify the treaty for the United States to join the League. Isolationism once again governed American foreign affairs.

Wilson's dreams of a peace that would end war was not to be. France and Great Britain desired that Germany be punished for the war that had claimed the lives of twenty million people around the globe. The Treaty of Versailles was negotiated and signed. Germany was humiliated: it had part of its land taken away and was forced to pay reparations to the countries it fought. Germany viewed this as an unfair admission of guilt for a war that it did not even begin. The other two losers of the war, Austria-Hungary and the Ottoman Empire, were dismembered. Broken into many smaller countries, they ceased to be world powers. Resentment in Germany would lead to the beginning of World War II just two decades later.

The Interwar Period

The time between the two world wars was largely marked by American isolationism. The country refused to join the League of Nations, turning its back on Europe. However, it did continue to control the Philippines and

Few events in the twentieth century were as important as the Russian Revolution. In 1917, the Russian Empire was engaged in World War I. Its armies were losing badly to Germany and Austria-Hungary. The tsar, Russia's monarch, was becoming more and more unpopular with each loss on the battlefield. Around that time, the Russian revolutionary Vladimir Lenin returned home. Lenin was a Communist who wanted to overthrow the monarchy. Communists believe that the means of production—farms and factories— should belong to the whole country rather than individuals. Lenin envisioned a single Communist party should run the government, rather than the multiparty system of representative government.

In 1917, the tsar was toppled from power. Soon after, Lenin and his Bolshevik party seized power from the new government. This led to a bloody civil war between the Communist and anti-Communist forces. The Allied powers, including the United States, sent soldiers to support anti-Communist forces. Nevertheless, Lenin and his supporters prevailed.

The Soviet Union was established in 1922. As the Allies had feared, it would later spread Communism beyond its borders. It also led to the Cold War between the United

Vladimir Lenin, the Russian revolutionary who founded the Soviet Union, was responsible for creating the first Communist state.

States, supported by other Western powers, and the Soviet Union. The seeds for this struggle were planted by the chaos and violence of World War I.

occupy countries like Nicaragua and Haiti in the Western Hemisphere. Even this period of isolationism did not see a full withdrawal of the United States from the world.

The inauguration of Franklin Delano Roosevelt in 1933 led to even greater isolationism. Roosevelt adopted the Good Neighbor Policy toward the nations of the Western Hemisphere. Abandoning the Roosevelt Corollary of his cousin Theodore Roosevelt, he renounced unilateral military interventions in the region. He ended the occupation of Nicaragua and Haiti. This noninterventionist American policy proved short-lived. After World War II, America's role in the world expanded like never before.

World War II

In 1931, Japan began expanding across Asia. The country had rapidly industrialized after Commodore Perry's expedition. Japan's military and economic power was unmatched in Asia. The Japanese government began to build a colonial empire in the European model, invading China.

In Europe, fascism reared its head. Fascists believed that the state should be ruled by a strong central government. They were also fervent nationalists, believing that their countries should expand. Furthermore, they were often convinced of their racial superiority. Benito Mussolini

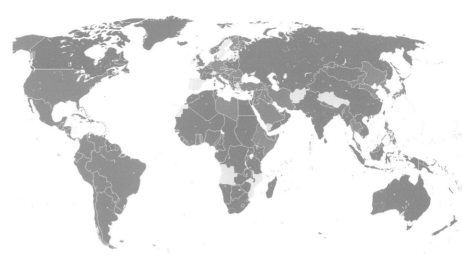

World War II involved most of the world. The blue countries fought on the side of the Axis, while the green countries made up the Allies.

seized power in Italy and became its dictator. In Germany, Adolf Hitler and his Nazi Party took control. Hitler began to take territory from his neighbors, and the League of Nations was unable to stop him peacefully. Japan, Italy, and Germany formed an alliance, known as the Axis. All three countries were totalitarian: the state wielded absolute power, and its interests were prioritized over those of individual citizens.

In 1939, Hitler invaded Poland. France and Great Britain came to Poland's defense. World War II had begun. Germany seized most of mainland Europe, including France. Great Britain kept fighting, but it was outmatched. The United States remained neutral. Its people and politicians had no appetite for another European war, and they were committed to isolationism.

Japanese forces attacked the Hawaiian military base of Pearl Harbor on December 7, 1941. In the fighting, 2,335 American military personnel were killed. But the Japanese failed in their objective to destroy the American Pacific fleet and prevent America from interfering in its conquest of Asia. Roosevelt declared it "a date that will live in infamy," and Congress declared war on Japan the next day. The United States had entered World War II. The war was seen as a struggle between totalitarianism on the side of the Axis and freedom and democracy on the side of Great Britain and the United States.

Hitler also invaded the Soviet Union in 1941, which opened the Eastern Front in Europe. While Germany initially saw some success, the Soviet Union put up stiff resistance. These events made the United States and Soviet Union unlikely allies in their fight against the Axis.

The United States began a campaign of island hopping across the Pacific. In need of airfields and supply bases, the US Marines took island after island in bloody, close-quarter fighting on small strips of beach. They were supported by the US Navy, which soon showed its superiority over the Japanese navy.

In Europe, the United States launched the D-Day Invasion of France on June 6, 1944. American soldiers

The battleship USS *Arizona* burns as it sinks after the attack on Pearl Harbor.

invaded from Great Britain into occupied France. The invasion opened a Western front with Germany, which was still fighting the Soviet Union on the Eastern Front. The German line began to crumble on both sides, and in 1945, the German capital of Berlin fell to Soviet forces. The war in Europe was over, but the war against Japan continued.

President Harry Truman made the decision to drop the atomic bomb on Japanese cities to bring the war to an end. Two bombs were dropped on Hiroshima and Nagasaki—the capital of Tokyo had already been destroyed by conventional bombs. More than two hundred thousand Japanese civilians were killed or wounded. Truman defended the decision on the basis that an invasion of Japan would have led to heavy American losses. Nonetheless, he came under criticism from some Americans who questioned the morality of purposefully killing large numbers of civilians. Japan surrendered after the unprecedented destruction and high civilian death toll of the bombings.

The United Nations

With the end of World War II, the League of Nations was replaced by the United Nations (UN). The two organizations shared many of the same objectives, like safeguarding peace, but the United Nations was meant to be more responsive to crises. It did not require unanimous support for a decision. The strongest body of the UN is the Security Council. It has five permanent members and ten temporary members (formerly, there was just five). The permanent members are the United States, Russia (formerly the Soviet Union), Great Britain, France, and China—the winners of World War II. The permanent members wield veto power, meaning that a single "no" vote from any of the five is enough to prevent the Security Council from acting.

The power to veto was necessary for the adoption of the UN. It allowed the major powers of the day to safeguard their interests. They were free to join the organization with little worry that it would be used against them. However, the veto also leads to frequent deadlock. This was especially true during the Cold War, when the United States and Soviet Union were at odds. Few significant acts on the world stage were acceptable to both parties.

Cities across Europe had to be rebuilt after the destruction of World War II. Pictured here is the historic German city of Dresden after an Allied bombing raid.

Chapter Four

The Cold War and American Dominance: 1945–present

★ ★ ★ ★ ★ ★ ★

The end of World War II set the stage for the Cold War that dominated the next four decades of American history. The wartime alliance between the United States and Soviet Union quickly soured. Their competing ideologies of democracy and communism would come into conflict across the world.

Rebuilding Europe and American Primacy

The world was left devasted by World War II. Europe was in shambles. Allied bombings and fierce battles had leveled cities across the continent. Japan was similarly left

★ ★ ★ ★ ★ ★ ★

in ruins by the atomic bombings as well as conventional bombings that had burned most of their cities to the ground. By comparison, the United States weathered the war much better. No foreign armies destroyed vast swaths of its territory. Less than half a million American military personnel died in the fighting. This was a massive loss of life, but far less than most other nations involved. As a result, the United States became the leading power of the world.

By comparison, the Soviet Union was devastated by World War II. Approximately twenty-four million Soviet soldiers and civilians lost their lives in the war: no country contributed more to the fight against fascism. Its economy could not match that of the United States, but unlike the United States, the Soviet Union did not scale back its military in the aftermath of the war. It seized Eastern Europe, formerly occupied by the Axis. When the war ended, the Soviet Union set up many communist states in Europe that were controlled from Moscow.

Much of the world was closely aligned with the Soviet Union or the United States. Japan and Western Europe were under American influence, and the United States set about helping them rebuild. The Marshall Plan saw the United States give more than $13 billion to Western Europe to improve its economy. Japan was occupied by the American military. A democratic government was installed, and its economy was rebuilt as well.

The United States spearheaded the creation of the North Atlantic Treaty Organization (NATO) in 1949. Originally twelve countries, the organization spread across Western Europe and into Asia with the inclusion of Turkey. Its members were committed to mutual defense. An attack on any member would be met by a military response from all. They formed a bulwark against further Soviet expansion. The collective security arrangement of NATO and American economic aid to democracies around the world was meant to contain Soviet influence.

The Cold War

The creation of the Eastern Bloc, led by the Soviet Union, and the Western Bloc, led by the United States, marked the beginning of the Cold War. This conflict was called the Cold War because Soviet and American forces never directly confronted each other in open war. It was a long-running conflict that historians typically date from 1947 to 1991. The two superpowers of the United States and the Soviet Union used proxy wars fought largely by other countries to battle each other. The threat of a nuclear exchange in the event of open war between the two superpowers helped prevent direct combat.

The Cold War shifted the American discourse on internationalism versus isolationism. Both Republicans and Democrats agreed that communism must be contained

The Truman Doctrine

On March 12, 1947, President Harry S. Truman delivered to Congress one of the most important speeches in American Cold War foreign policy. He outlined a vision of the world as divided between two ways of life:

One way of life is based upon the will of the majority, and is distinguished by free institutions, representative government, free elections, guarantees of individual liberty, freedom of speech and religion, and freedom from political oppression.

The second way of life is based upon the will of a minority forcibly imposed upon the majority. It relies upon terror and oppression, a controlled press and radio; fixed elections, and the suppression of personal freedoms.

Additionally, Truman laid out the American strategy of containment that would play a pivotal role in the conflict:

I believe that it must be the policy of the United States to support free peoples who are resisting attempted subjugation by armed minorities or by outside pressures.

Harry S. Truman served as president at the end of World War II and the beginning of the Cold War.

> I believe that we must assist free peoples to work out their own destinies in their own way.
> I believe that our help should be primarily through economic and financial aid which is essential to economic stability and orderly political processes.

Containment meant that Soviet expansion would be stopped. Truman's speech focused on the use of economic and financial aid to contain the Soviet Union. Later, he and the presidents who followed him would expand the strategy to include direct military action by the United States.

through aggressive intervention in foreign affairs. The isolationism of George Washington's farewell address faded from view. The United States was firmly committed to having a strong presence internationally.

The Cold War strategy of containment varied in its methods. Sometimes, the United States adopted an aggressive stance, waging wars in foreign countries and confronting the Soviet Union on the world stage. Other periods were marked by détente—a relaxing of tensions between the two countries. The two sides were able to compromise on some issues, such as limiting the number of nuclear weapons on both sides.

The Korean War

While the Cold War never saw Soviet and American armies meet in battle, many American soldiers saw combat around the world in wars that were part of the larger Cold War struggle. The first major American military action of the Cold War was in Korea. The country had been occupied by the Japanese during World War II. After the war, it was partitioned with a communist regime in the North and an American-backed dictator in the South.

North Korea launched a surprise attack on South Korea in 1950 with the approval of Joseph Stalin, the leader of the Soviet Union. South Korean forces were unable to stop North Korea's advance and were in danger of losing the war when President Truman decided to intervene and try to contain the spread of communism. He obtained the support of the United Nations, and American soldiers were sent to the country to intervene. The Soviet Union was boycotting the UN at the time, so it did not use its veto power to oppose Truman.

The American military saw early successes against North Korean forces. They took the capital of North Korea and were approaching the Chinese border when the situation suddenly changed. China had a communist government under Mao Zedong. When the United States ignored China's warning to stay well away from the border, Chinese soldiers poured across and engaged American forces. Vastly outnumbered, the Americans retreated. After the capital of South Korea was lost once again, and then retaken, the battle lines stabilized near the original partition line between North and South.

In 1953, an armistice was signed that ended the fighting. Nevertheless, no peace treaty was ever signed, and the conflict officially continues. North and South Korea are still separated by the demilitarized zone (DMZ)—a heavily secured border with land mines, barbed wire, and soldiers stationed on both sides. The war had no clear victor, but communism was contained. It also set a precedent of aggressive American military response in the Cold War. Today, it is called the Forgotten War, but

Korea's mountainous terrain and sometimes bitterly cold weather caused great difficulties for soldiers.

thirty-six thousand American military personnel gave their lives in the conflict. Their sacrifice is remembered and honored in South Korea, which eventually gained a democratic government.

The Vietnam War

Vietnam was the second country that the United States went to war to defend. It had been a French colony before being occupied by the Japanese army during World War II. After the war ended, France regained control. However, there was now a strong, armed, nationalist movement for an independent Vietnam, which had resisted the Japanese with force. They were called the Viet Minh, and they began to fight the French. France was no longer the great power it had been before World War II, and it was forced to withdraw after a costly military defeat in 1954.

The United States' Role in the World

Vietnam was partitioned between the Viet Minh in the north and a pro-Western government in the south. Crucially, the Viet Minh were not only a nationalist group, but also communist. This led to the gradual involvement of the United States in the conflict. Communist guerrillas took the fight to South Vietnam, and the United States began to send financial aid and military advisors to contain communism to the north.

US involvement eventually expanded to bombing North Vietnam and then to the involvement of American soldiers in battles on the ground in 1965. Direct American military involvement lasted until 1973. Despite American military superiority, South Vietnam fell in 1975. The United States was forced to withdraw from the war after sustaining heavy losses. During the war, fifty-eight thousand Americans died. Up to two million Vietnamese soldiers on both sides, as well as many civilians, died in the conflict.

This grim death toll on all sides led to a strong antiwar protest movement in the United States. For the first time, the Cold War strategy of aggressive containment through direct military involvement was truly challenged. The Vietnam War was a watershed moment in American history. By its end, it was a deeply unpopular war. The American government was found to have lied about several key facts. At the same time, President Richard Nixon resigned due to a political scandal, the Watergate scandal. Americans' trust in the government was weakened, and the government's relationship with the media never fully recovered from the many lies of the Vietnam War era. Today, the Vietnam War is still cited as an example of what can go wrong when the United States intervenes abroad.

The Reagan Doctrine

In 1981, Ronald Reagan was elected as president of the United States. The conservative Republican ran on a platform of strong national defense. After taking office, he outlined his vision of a new foreign policy: the Reagan Doctrine. Rather than contain communism like the presidents before him, he wanted to drive it out of countries across the world.

To do this, Reagan's administrations intervened in numerous nations around the world. The US government sent arms to Afghanistan, which was being invaded by the Soviet Union. They supported rebel groups in Angola and Nicaragua—two countries with communist governments. It was a marked shift in American foreign policy to intervene more frequently. Nonetheless, Reagan only sent American soldiers to one foreign war: the quickly-won invasion of the small Caribbean island of Grenada.

Reagan's interventions drew heavy criticism from some Americans and many foreign powers. The anticommunist groups he supported frequently violated human rights. In the Cold War, the United States often decided to support totalitarian governments and violent rebels whose fight against communism aligned with American interests. Supporting the values of freedom and democracy abroad was deemed less important than the struggle against communism.

Ronald Reagan's administration intervened in many countries with the aim of ending communism.

The Reagan Doctrine's influence did not end when Reagan left the presidency after two terms. It was incorporated into the foreign policy of his successors. Even after the Cold War ended, the United States was much more willing to intervene in foreign countries than before he took office.

The Last Superpower

Reagan's confrontation of the Soviet Union helped bring about the end of the Cold War. He opposed the regime in a number of high-profile speeches. He famously stood before the Berlin Wall, the symbolic divider of the eastern and western blocs, and said, "Mr. Gorbachev, tear down this wall!" Mikhail Gorbachev was the leader of the Soviet Union at its end.

Reagan also ramped up American military spending. When the Soviet Union tried to do the same, it became clear that the superpower could not in fact match the United States. Its economy was struggling, and its people were disillusioned with their government. In 1991, Gorbachev oversaw the breakup of the Soviet Union into fifteen independent countries. The countries abandoned communism and reformed their economies. They adopted varying levels of representative government, although dictators took power in some.

With the breakup of the Soviet Union, the world's balance of power shifted. It was no longer a bipolar world with the United States and Soviet Union at the two poles. Instead, it was a unipolar international system: American supremacy was unchallenged.

The era of frequent American interventions did not end with the Cold War. President George H. W. Bush launched the Gulf War against Iraq when Iraq invaded the small neighboring country of Kuwait. Bush envisioned a "new world order" with the United States leading a multinational coalition to respond to threats.

The War on Terror

On September 11, 2001, the worst terrorist attack on American soil took place. Four passenger jets were hijacked

Humanitarian Interventions

President George H. W. Bush and his successor, Bill Clinton, oversaw a number of humanitarian interventions in the new unipolar international system. A humanitarian intervention is when the military is used to end crimes against humanity, like mass killings. Bush and Clinton both sent peacekeepers to Somalia during its civil war. They hoped to stabilize the country so that famine relief aid could be distributed. However, American soldiers were withdrawn after nineteen died during the mission that inspired the book and movie *Black Hawk Down*.

The breakup of the country of Yugoslavia also witnessed an American intervention. In 1999, Clinton led a NATO bombing campaign amid reports of government crimes. This intervention was controversial because Russia and China opposed it. Clinton decided to go ahead with the operation even without the United Nations' approval.

In 1991, the African country of Rwanda suffered a genocide in which eight hundred thousand people were killed because of their ethnicity. Clinton decided not to intervene, although he later said this was one of the greatest regrets of his presidency.

The decision of whether to intervene in a foreign humanitarian crisis is difficult. The question of what to do in these circumstances can define a president's foreign policy legacy.

and deliberately crashed into buildings on the ground. Two were flown into the Twin Towers of the World Trade Center in New York City. One hit the Pentagon in Arlington, Virginia—the headquarters of the Department of Defense. The fourth hijacked plane was forced down by its passengers when they heard of the earlier attacks. Close to three thousand victims died on September 11.

The United States' government quickly determined that Osama bin Laden, the leader of the terrorist group al-Qaeda, was responsible. He was being harbored by another terror organization, the Taliban, in Afghanistan. When the Taliban refused to hand him over, President George W. Bush led the invasion of Afghanistan. He was supported by a broad multinational coalition, including NATO. While the initial takeover of the country was quick, bin Laden escaped.

At the same time, Bush looked to Iraq. He labeled Iraq as a state sponsor of terror even though it had no connection to the September 11 terror attack. The American government accused Iraq of stockpiling weapons of mass destruction—chemical, biological, or nuclear weapons. It later turned out this claim was false, but in 2003, the United States invaded Iraq. This time, few allies joined the American effort. Most countries regarded American claims of weapons of mass destruction with skepticism.

The wars in Iraq and Afghanistan dragged on for many years. Insurgencies—military resistance to the presence

American soldiers operate in Iraq during the opening days of the American invasion.

of American soldiers—developed in both countries. Iraq descended into a civil war between rival factions with American troops targeted by both sides. The American-backed governments were unpopular and corrupt.

The wars were also controversial at home. Americans grew to oppose the conflicts as more Americans died, and it was revealed that the reason for invading Iraq was overstated by the Bush administration. In 2011, American soldiers finally withdrew from Iraq. In 2014, major combat operations in Afghanistan ended, although some troops remained for counterterrorism operations and to advise the Afghan forces.

Bush's decision to invade Iraq was important to American foreign policy. He largely ignored the precedent of other post-Cold War presidents that focused on coalition building and multinational forces. With few allies—other than Great Britain—willing to help in Iraq, Bush acted unilaterally. Bush also hoped to spread democracy across the Middle East and undermine terrorism in the future. His administration believed terrorism grew from a lack of freedom. The idea of spreading democracy is as old as the United States, but Bush was notable in trying to do so through major military operations abroad.

The Obama Doctrine

Bush's successor as president, Barack Obama, also changed the foreign policy of the United States. Obama was responsible for ending the war in Iraq as well as ending major combat operations in Afghanistan—after a brief surge in troop levels dealt a major blow to the insurgency.

Obama's administration believed that the United States could act unilaterally to defend its interests, but in general interventions should be multinational. He expanded the use of unmanned aerial vehicles—drones—in bombing terrorist targets around the globe. The use of drones was considered vital to national security.

When it came to humanitarian interventions, Obama first assembled a broad multinational coalition. This

In the foreground of this photograph, a predator drone carrying Hellfire missiles lands after a mission. Thousands of American drone strikes have taken place since the first one in 2004.

prevented criticism from close American allies, a defining feature of the Iraq War. One of the greatest challenges of Obama's tenure was the Arab Spring, a wave of prodemocracy protests that swept across the Middle East beginning in 2010. Some governments were overthrown peacefully, but Syria and Libya descended into civil war when the governments of those nations met protesters with violence.

Obama assembled a coalition to intervene in Libya through airstrikes. The strikes supported rebels that opposed the dictator Muammar Qaddafi. France and

Great Britain joined the effort, and Qaddafi was eventually killed by rebel forces on the ground. Nonetheless, Libya descended into civil war and political chaos. Obama's intervention was later criticized by many, although he defended his decision to act.

In Syria, dictator Bashar al-Assad was also challenged by rebel forces in 2011. The United States sent aid to rebel groups but did not immediately get involved. When an al-Qaeda affiliate, the Islamic State in Iraq and Syria (ISIS), began to gain large stretches of territory in 2014, the United States once again led a coalition to fight back with airstrikes. In 2017, the bombing campaign was expanding to the forces of Assad. As of late 2018, the Syrian Civil War continues. The United States backs some rebels, others are terrorist groups, and the government is heavily supported by Russia, which leads its own bombing campaign in the country.

Nuclear Ambitions

One of the greatest foreign policy issues of the present day is nuclear proliferation. Currently, there are five states with internationally sanctioned nuclear arsenals: the United States, Russia, China, Great Britain, and France. India, Pakistan, and North Korea also have nuclear weapons with varying degrees of international approval.

North Korea is the one country with nuclear weapons that is internationally sanctioned as a result. Sanctions are penalties applied to a nation by other countries. The United Nations has condemned the North Korean government repeatedly due to its nuclear weapons program. For years, presidents have tried to negotiate with North Korea so the country will give up its nuclear arsenal.

Iran was pursuing a nuclear program until 2015, although the nation claimed it was strictly for nuclear energy. In 2015, a deal was struck between Iran and world powers. It would restrict its nuclear program, and in return sanctions would be lifted. But in 2018, Donald Trump unilaterally announced that the United States was withdrawing from the deal even though the United States had helped negotiate it under the Obama administration. Trump pushed for renewed sanctions against Iran—a clear violation of the deal's terms. The other signatories to the deal remain committed to it, but it is unclear if the deal can survive. Iran has threatened to start its nuclear program again if sanctions are put back in place.

The problem of disarming North Korea and preventing Iran from developing nuclear weapons is one of the most pressing debates in American foreign policy. There is a divide between those who think that negotiation and deals are the answer versus those that look to force and threats.

A Continuing Debate

Throughout American history, the tension between isolationism and intervention has been strong. Early in American history, isolationism often won out, although there were many exceptions, including westward expansion, American imperialism, and involvement in both World Wars. Since World War II, isolationism has largely faded from public conversation. The United States is deeply committed to a large footprint abroad with military bases in many nations and involvement in numerous ongoing conflicts like those in Syria and Afghanistan.

Both Democrats and Republicans are committed to a world where the United States plays an integral role on the world stage. As the sole superpower, America often takes the lead in multinational efforts. Debates over American involvement often center around acting unilaterally or as the leader of a multinational coalition. The idea that the United States would withdraw completely from the world stage, common before both world wars, is now absent. Opposition to deep involvement in world affairs is currently restricted to politicians outside the political mainstream.

At the same time, the presidency of Donald Trump has shifted the public discourse to a limited extent. Trump has remained committed to a large military presence abroad and interventions in foreign conflicts. However, he has cast doubt on free trade, an ideal that had defined most of American history. Trump has suggested that free trade is not in the United States' economic interests. He went so far as to withdraw from the Trans-Pacific Partnership (TPP), a massive trade agreement negotiated by Obama.

Critics argue that the withdrawal from the TPP limited American influence in Asia. This relates to what many consider the greatest threat to American power—the rise of China. China's economy is expected to surpass that of the United States around 2030. This is due to its large population and rapid economic growth. Some politicians worry this will change the current unipolar international system. China may become a player equal to the United States. Nevertheless, it is unlikely that China will have a military that can equal the United States in the near future. China has also been hesitant to intervene in foreign conflicts, preferring peaceful development.

Currently, America's role as the world's sole superpower looks secure. It is up to the American public to decide how involved the country should be in world affairs and foreign conflicts. The question of how to balance the aggressive defense of national interests with the American ideals of peace and democracy is also pressing. These challenges have shaped American history and remain central to America's role in the world today.

★ CHRONOLOGY ★

October 12, 1492

> Christopher Columbus makes landfall in the
> Americas, sparking the European colonization of the
> New World.

February 10, 1763

> The French and Indian War ends, and the thirteen
> colonies gain territory west to the Mississippi River.

July 4, 1776

> The Declaration of Independence is approved,
> and the thirteen colonies are no longer part of
> Great Britain.

September 19, 1796

> George Washington urges his countrymen to
> avoid entanglements in European affairs in his
> farewell address.

May 2, 1803

> The Louisiana Purchase doubles the size of the
> United States.

June 8, 1812

> The United States declares war on Great Britain, beginning the War of 1812, which ends with no concessions by either side.

December 2, 1823

> James Monroe articulates the Monroe Doctrine, which says the United States will not approve of further European interventions in the Western Hemisphere.

February 2, 1848

> The Mexican-American War ends with a large territorial gain by the United States.

July 7, 1898

> Hawaii is annexed by the United States.

December 10, 1898

> The Spanish-American War ends, and the United States gains control of the Philippines, Cuba, Puerto Rico, and Guam.

April 6, 1917

> The United States declares war on Germany and joins World War I.

January 10, 1920

> The League of Nations is formed, but US Congress refuses to join the international effort.

December 7, 1941

> The Japanese bomb the American port of Pearl Harbor. The United States enters World War II as a result.

October 24, 1945

> The United Nations is formed. The United States becomes a permanent member of the Security Council.

March 12, 1947

> Harry S. Truman outlines the Truman Doctrine of containing the Soviet Union to its current borders.

June 25, 1950

> North Korea invades South Korea, and American forces join the war to contain the spread of communism.

March 29, 1973

> The United States withdraws combat troops from Vietnam after eight years of warfare in the country.

February 6, 1985

> Ronald Reagan announces the Reagan Doctrine of rolling back the Soviet Union through foreign intervention.

The United States' Role in the World

September 11, 2001

> The United States suffers the deadliest terror attack on its soil in history.

October 7, 2001

> The United States invades Afghanistan in response to the September 11 terror attack.

March 20, 2003

> The United States invades Iraq after mistakenly accusing it of stockpiling weapons of mass destruction.

December 2010

> The Arab Spring begins, and the United States is forced to react.

January 23, 2017

> The United States withdraws from the Trans-Pacific Partnership—a major trade agreement.

May 8, 2018

> Donald Trump announces that the United States will no longer abide by the Iran nuclear deal it helped negotiate in 2015.

GLOSSARY

belligerent A nation taking part in a conflict.

bicameral legislature A legislature with two different chambers. In the United States, these are the Senate and the House of Representatives.

capitalism The economic system of the United States whereby the means of production, like farms and factories, are owned by individuals and not the state.

communism The economic system of the Soviet Union where the means of production, like farms and factories, are strictly controlled by the state and not by individual citizens.

Enlightenment A European movement of the late seventeenth and eighteenth centuries. It saw the celebration of reason, the separation of church and state, and personal freedom gain popularity even while Europe was ruled by kings and queens.

expansionism The policy of expanding a nation's territory, often at the expense of its neighbors or overseas countries.

imperialism The policy of expanding a nation's territory or influence through military conquest or other means, such as diplomatic or economic pressure.

internationalism The practice of collaboration and closer relationships among different nations.

interventionism The practice of intervening in the affairs of foreign countries.

isolationism A policy of withdrawal from world affairs, including foreign wars and alliances.

precedent An action or decision that acts as a model for future action.

sovereignty The ability of a nation to govern itself.

textile Relating to fabric.

ultimatum A demand that a nation must act in some way or face consequences.

unilateral One-sided.

★ FURTHER INFORMATION ★

★ ★ ★ ★ ★ ★ ★

Books

Brownell, Richard. *The Cold War*. Farmington Hills, MI: Lucent Books, 2009.

Merino, Noel. *US Foreign Policy*. Farmington Hills, MI: Greenhaven Publishing, 2015.

Renehan, Edward J. *The Monroe Doctrine: The Cornerstone of American Foreign Policy*. New York: Facts on File, 2007.

Websites

Explore WWII History

https://www.nationalww2museum.org/students-teachers/student-resources/explore-wwii-history

The National World War II Museum presents a number of articles and features related to America's role in World War II.

Westward Expansion, 1790–1850

https://www.pbslearningmedia.org/resource/rttt12.soc.ush.westexp/westward-expansion-17901850/#.Wxhg3I6n9Sl

PBS provides an interactive map of American expansion west.

★ ★ ★ ★ ★ ★ ★

Videos

America in World War I: Crash Course US History #30

https://www.youtube.com/watch?v=y59wErqg4Xg

The Crash Course team explores United States' involvement in World War I.

How America Became a Superpower

https://www.youtube.com/watch?v=BShvYeYMm_Y

Vox describes the growth of the United States and its role in the international system.

Third Presidential Debate – What is America's Role in the World

https://www.youtube.com/watch?v=3-_tshTFgNQ

During a 2012 presidential debate, Barack Obama and Mitt Romney give their answers to the question, "What is America's Role in the World?"

★ BIBLIOGRAPHY ★

Bellamy, Jay. "The Zimmerman Telegram." *Prologue* 48, no. 4 (Winter 2016). https://www.archives.gov/publications/prologue/2016/winter/zimmermann-telegram.

Doyle, Don. "How the Civil War Changed the World." *New York Times*, May 19, 2005. https://opinionator.blogs.nytimes.com/2015/05/19/how-the-civil-war-changed-the-world.

Gaddis, John Lewis. *The Cold War: A New History*. New York: Penguin Books, 2006.

Guelzo, Allan C. *Lincoln's Emancipation Proclamation: The End of Slavery in America*. New York: Simon & Schuster, 2006.

Hickey, Donald. "An American Perspective on the War of 1812." PBS. Retrieved May 26, 2018. http://www.pbs.org/wned/war-of-1812/essays/american-perspective.

Joyner, James. "Obama Doctrine, Reagan Doctrine." *National Interest*, January 18, 2013. http://nationalinterest.org/commentary/obama-doctrine-reagan-doctrine-7982.

Knott, Stephen. "George H. W. Bush: Foreign Affairs." The Miller Center. Retrieved May 26, 2018. https://millercenter.org/president/bush/foreign-affairs.

Rosenfeld, Stephen S. "The Reagan Doctrine: The Guns of July." *Foreign Policy*, Spring 1986. https://www. foreignaffairs.com/articles/1986-03-01/reagan-doctrine-guns-july.

Sargent, Daniel. "American Foreign Economic Policy." *Oxford Research Encyclopedia of American History*. Retrieved May 26, 2018. http://americanhistory.oxfordre.com/ view/10.1093/acrefore/9780199329175.001.0001/ acrefore-9780199329175-e-52.

Savage, Charlie. "Attack Renews Debate over Congressional Assent." *New York Times*, March 21, 2011. https://www. nytimes.com/2011/03/22/world/africa/22powers.html.

Scott, Malcolm, and Cedric Sam. "Here's How Fast China's Economy is Catching up to the U.S." *Bloomberg*, May 12, 2016. https://www.bloomberg.com/graphics/2016-us-vs-china-economy.

Yoo, John. "George Washington and the Executive Power." *University of St. Thomas Journal of Law & Public Policy* 5, no. 1 (2010): 1–35.

Zenko, Micah. "The Slippery Slope of U.S. Intervention." *Foreign Policy*, August 12, 2014. http://foreignpolicy. com/2014/08/12/the-slippery-slope-of-u-s-intervention.

★ INDEX ★

★ ABOUT THE AUTHOR ★

Derek Miller is a writer and educator from Salisbury, Maryland. He is the author of numerous books for young readers, including *Peaceful Protesters: Henry David Thoreau*, *Focus on Africa: The Economy in Contemporary Africa*, and *Routes of Cross-Cultural Exchange: The Silk Road*. When he is not writing or teaching, Miller enjoys traveling with his wife.

THIS BOOK IS SAFARI ENABLED

INCLUDES FREE 45-DAY ACCESS TO THE ONLINE EDITION

The Safari® Enabled icon on the cover of your favorite technology book means the book is available through Safari Bookshelf. When you buy this book, you get free access to the online edition for 45 days.

Safari Bookshelf is an electronic reference library that lets you easily search thousands of technical books, find code samples, download chapters, and access technical information whenever and wherever you need it.

TO GAIN 45-DAY SAFARI ENABLED ACCESS TO THIS BOOK:

- Go to **http://www.quepublishing.com/safarienabled**
- Complete the brief registration form
- Enter the coupon code found in the front of this book on page v

If you have difficulty registering on Safari Bookshelf or accessing the online edition, please e-mail customer-service@safaribooksonline.com.

Safari Library
Subscribe Now!

http://safari.informit.com/library

Safari's entire technology collection is now available with no restrictions. Imagine the value of being able to search and access thousands of books, videos, and articles from leading technology authors whenever you wish.

EXPLORE TOPICS MORE FULLY

Gain a more robust understanding of related issues by using Safari as your research tool. With Safari Library you can leverage the knowledge of the world's technology gurus. For one flat, monthly fee, you'll have unrestricted access to a reference collection offered nowhere else in the world—all at your fingertips.

With a Safari Library subscription, you'll get the following premium services:

- **Immediate access to the newest, cutting-edge books**—Approximately eighty new titles are added per month in conjunction with, or in advance of, their print publication.

- **Chapter downloads**—Download five chapters per month so you can work offline when you need to.

- **Rough Cuts**—A service that provides online access to prepublication information on advanced technologies. Content is updated as the author writes the book. You can also download Rough Cuts for offline reference

- **Videos**—Premier design and development videos from training and e-learning expert lynda.com and other publishers you trust.

- **Cut and paste code**—Cut and paste code directly from Safari. Save time. Eliminate errors.

- **Save up to 35% on print books**—Safari Subscribers receive a discount of up to 35% on publishers' print books.

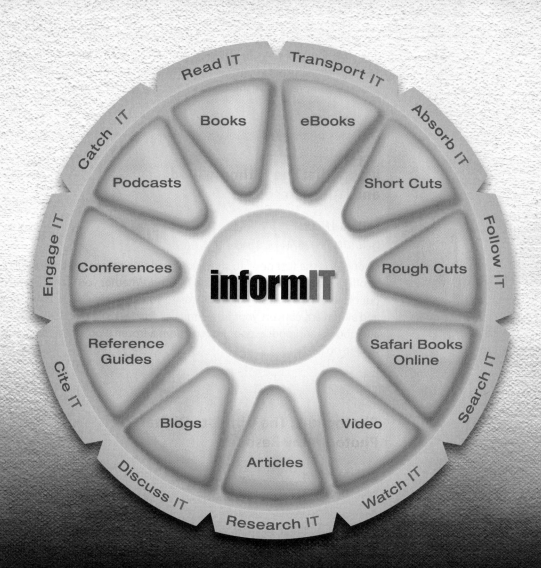

Check out these interesting titles!

Googlepedia: The Ultimate Google Resource, Second Edition

By Michael Miller
ISBN: 9780789736758 | 864 pages

Googlepedia is not just for searching! Did you know that over the years Google has added a variety of features, services, tools, and businesses that make it a one-stop-shop for virtually any web user? This book takes you way beyond web searches by exposing you to Google's tools, services, and features. *Googlepedia* provides comprehensive information that will benefit every Google user.

iPodpedia: The Ultimate iPod and iTunes Resource

By Michael Miller
ISBN: 9780789736741 | 528 pages

iPodpedia is the first book to show you everything that iPod and iTunes have to offer—from music to movies and beyond. Whether you want to get the most out of your iPod's music playback, create your own playlists, edit your music info and album art, convert your home movies and DVDs to iPod videos, listen to audiobooks and podcasts, or just unfreeze a frozen iPod, *iPodpedia* will tell you how to do it.

Photopedia: The Ultimate Digital Photography Resource

By Michael Miller
ISBN: 9780789737250 | 624 pages

Photopedia is a comprehensive A to Z guide that includes instruction in both basic photographic techniques and advanced digital image manipulation. This is a full-color guide to all aspects of digital photography—from composing the shot to editing, printing, or sharing the photograph. *Photopedia* is perfect for those new to digital photography and for traditional photographers who face a learning curve when switching to digital.

Look for these books at retailers everywhere
or visit informit.com/que to buy your copy today!

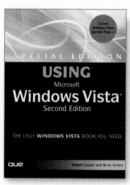